MW00855864

Sermons
To
Remember

By
Michael & Felicia Cole

Dedication:

To the Lord Jesus Christ who gave us the revelation and knowledge to complete this book.

Acknowledgement:

To Pat McLaughlin and Donald Terry for sharing their insight and knowledge.

Abbreviations for The Books of the Bible
The Old Testament

Book	Abbreviation	Book	Abbreviation
Genesis	Gen	Ecclesiastes	Eccl
Exodus	Ex	Songs of Solomon	Song
Leviticus	Lev	Isaiah	Isa
Numbers	Num	Jeremiah	Jer
Deuteronomy	Dt	Lamentations	Lam
Joshua	Josh	Ezekiel	Ezek
Judges	Jud	Daniel	Dan
Ruth	Ruth	Hosea	Hos
1 Samuel	1 Sam	Joel	Joel
2 Samuel	2 Sam	Amos	Amos
1 Kings	1 Ki	Obadiah	Obad
2 Kings	2 Ki	Jonah	Jon
1 Chronicles	1 Chr	Micah	Mic
2 Chronicles	2 Chr	Nahum	Nah
Ezra	Ezra	Habakkuk	Hab
Nehemiah	Neh	Zephaniah	Zeph
Esther	Est	Haggai	Hag
Job	Job	Zechariah	Zech
Psalms	Ps	Malachi	Mal
Proverbs	Prov		

The New Testament

Book	Abbreviation	Book	Abbreviation
Matthew	Mt	1 Timothy	1 Tim
Mark	Mk	2 Timothy	2 Tim
Luke	Lk	Titus	Ti
John	Jn	Philemon	Phile
Acts	Acts	Hebrews	Heb
Romans	Rom	James	Jas
1 Corinthians	1 Cor	1 Peter	1 Pet
2 Corinthians	2 Cor	2 Peter	2 Pet
Galatians	Gal	1 John	1 Jn
Ephesians	Eph	2 John	2 Jn
Philippians	Phil	2 John	3 Jn
Colossians	Col	Jude	Jude
1 Thessalonians	1 Th	Revelation	Rev
2 Thessalonians	2 Th		

*And this is life eternal, that they might
know thee the only true God
and Jesus Christ whom thou has sent.*
St. John 17:3

*I will praise thee, O Lord, with my
whole heart; I will show forth all thy
marvelous works.*

*I will be glad and rejoice in thee: I will
sing praise to thy name, O thou most
High.*
Psalm 9:1-2

2008

JANUARY
WK	S	M	T	W	T	F	S
1			1	2	3	4	5
2	6	7	8	9	10	11	12
3	13	14	15	16	17	18	19
4	20	21	22	23	24	25	26
5	27	28	29	30	31		

FEBRUARY
WK	S	M	T	W	T	F	S
5						1	2
6	3	4	5	6	7	8	9
7	10	11	12	13	14	15	16
8	17	18	19	20	21	22	23
9	24	25	26	27	28	29	

MARCH
WK	S	M	T	W	T	F	S
9							1
10	2	3	4	5	6	7	8
11	9	10	11	12	13	14	15
12	16	17	18	19	20	21	22
13	23	24	25	26	27	28	29
14	30	31					

APRIL
WK	S	M	T	W	T	F	S
14			1	2	3	4	5
15	6	7	8	9	10	11	12
16	13	14	15	16	17	18	19
17	20	21	22	23	24	25	26
18	27	28	29	30			

MAY
WK	S	M	T	W	T	F	S
18					1	2	3
19	4	5	6	7	8	9	10
20	11	12	13	14	15	16	17
21	18	19	20	21	22	23	24
22	25	26	27	28	29	30	31

JUNE
WK	S	M	T	W	T	F	S
23	1	2	3	4	5	6	7
24	8	9	10	11	12	13	14
25	15	16	17	18	19	20	21
26	22	23	24	25	26	27	28
27	29	30					

JULY
WK	S	M	T	W	T	F	S
27			1	2	3	4	5
28	6	7	8	9	10	11	12
29	13	14	15	16	17	18	19
30	20	21	22	23	24	25	26
31	27	28	29	30	31		

AUGUST
WK	S	M	T	W	T	F	S
31						1	2
32	3	4	5	6	7	8	9
33	10	11	12	13	14	15	16
34	17	18	19	20	21	22	23
35	24	25	26	27	28	29	30
36	31						

SEPTEMBER
WK	S	M	T	W	T	F	S
36		1	2	3	4	5	6
37	7	8	9	10	11	12	13
38	14	15	16	17	18	19	20
39	21	22	23	24	25	26	27
40	28	29	30				

OCTOBER
WK	S	M	T	W	T	F	S
40				1	2	3	4
41	5	6	7	8	9	10	11
42	12	13	14	15	16	17	18
43	19	20	21	22	23	24	25
44	26	27	28	29	30	31	

NOVEMBER
WK	S	M	T	W	T	F	S
44							1
45	2	3	4	5	6	7	8
46	9	10	11	12	13	14	15
47	16	17	18	19	20	21	22
48	23	24	25	26	27	28	29
49	30						

DECEMBER
WK	S	M	T	W	T	F	S
49		1	2	3	4	5	6
50	7	8	9	10	11	12	13
51	14	15	16	17	18	19	20
52	21	22	23	24	25	26	27
53	28	29	30	31			

2009

JANUARY
WK	S	M	T	W	T	F	S
1					1	2	3
2	4	5	6	7	8	9	10
3	11	12	13	14	15	16	17
4	18	19	20	21	22	23	24
5	25	26	27	28	29	30	31

FEBRUARY
WK	S	M	T	W	T	F	S
5	1	2	3	4	5	6	7
6	8	9	10	11	12	13	14
7	15	16	17	18	19	20	21
8	22	23	24	25	26	27	28

MARCH
WK	S	M	T	W	T	F	S
9	1	2	3	4	5	6	7
10	8	9	10	11	12	13	14
11	15	16	17	18	19	20	21
12	22	23	24	25	26	27	28
13	29	30	31				

APRIL
WK	S	M	T	W	T	F	S
13				1	2	3	4
14	5	6	7	8	9	10	11
15	12	13	14	15	16	17	18
16	19	20	21	22	23	24	25
17	26	27	28	29	30		

MAY
WK	S	M	T	W	T	F	S
17						1	2
18	3	4	5	6	7	8	9
19	10	11	12	13	14	15	16
20	17	18	19	20	21	22	23
21	24	25	26	27	28	29	30
22	31						

JUNE
WK	S	M	T	W	T	F	S
22		1	2	3	4	5	6
23	7	8	9	10	11	12	13
24	14	15	16	17	18	19	20
25	21	22	23	24	25	26	27
26	28	29	30				

JULY
WK	S	M	T	W	T	F	S
26				1	2	3	4
27	5	6	7	8	9	10	11
28	12	13	14	15	16	17	18
29	19	20	21	22	23	24	25
30	26	27	28	29	30	31	

AUGUST
WK	S	M	T	W	T	F	S
30							1
31	2	3	4	5	6	7	8
32	9	10	11	12	13	14	15
33	16	17	18	19	20	21	22
34	23	24	25	26	27	28	29
35	30	31					

SEPTEMBER
WK	S	M	T	W	T	F	S
35			1	2	3	4	5
36	6	7	8	9	10	11	12
37	13	14	15	16	17	18	19
38	20	21	22	23	24	25	26
39	27	28	29	30			

OCTOBER
WK	S	M	T	W	T	F	S
39					1	2	3
40	4	5	6	7	8	9	10
41	11	12	13	14	15	16	17
42	18	19	20	21	22	23	24
43	25	26	27	28	29	30	31

NOVEMBER
WK	S	M	T	W	T	F	S
44	1	2	3	4	5	6	7
45	8	9	10	11	12	13	14
46	15	16	17	18	19	20	21
47	22	23	24	25	26	27	28
48	29	30					

DECEMBER
WK	S	M	T	W	T	F	S
48			1	2	3	4	5
49	6	7	8	9	10	11	12
50	13	14	15	16	17	18	19
51	20	21	22	23	24	25	26
52	27	28	29	30	31		

2010

JANUARY
WK	S	M	T	W	T	F	S
1						1	2
2	3	4	5	6	7	8	9
3	10	11	12	13	14	15	16
4	17	18	19	20	21	22	23
5	24	25	26	27	28	29	30
6	31						

FEBRUARY
WK	S	M	T	W	T	F	S
6		1	2	3	4	5	6
7	7	8	9	10	11	12	13
8	14	15	16	17	18	19	20
9	21	22	23	24	25	26	27
10	28						

MARCH
WK	S	M	T	W	T	F	S
10		1	2	3	4	5	6
11	7	8	9	10	11	12	13
12	14	15	16	17	18	19	20
13	21	22	23	24	25	26	27
14	28	29	30	31			

APRIL
WK	S	M	T	W	T	F
14					1	2
15	4	5	6	7	8	9
16	11	12	13	14	15	16
17	18	19	20	21	22	23
18	25	26	27	28	29	30

MAY
WK	S	M	T	W	T	F	S
18							1
19	2	3	4	5	6	7	8
20	9	10	11	12	13	14	15
21	16	17	18	19	20	21	22
22	23	24	25	26	27	28	29
23	30	31					

JUNE
WK	S	M	T	W	T	F	S
23			1	2	3	4	5
24	6	7	8	9	10	11	12
25	13	14	15	16	17	18	19
26	20	21	22	23	24	25	26
27	27	28	29	30			

JULY
WK	S	M	T	W	T	F	S
27					1	2	3
28	4	5	6	7	8	9	10
29	11	12	13	14	15	16	17
30	18	19	20	21	22	23	24
31	25	26	27	28	29	30	31

AUGUST
WK	S	M	T	W	T	F
32	1	2	3	4	5	6
33	8	9	10	11	12	13
34	15	16	17	18	19	20
35	22	23	24	25	26	27
36	29	30	31			

SEPTEMBER
WK	S	M	T	W	T	F	S
36				1	2	3	4
37	5	6	7	8	9	10	11
38	12	13	14	15	16	17	18
39	19	20	21	22	23	24	25
40	26	27	28	29	30		

OCTOBER
WK	S	M	T	W	T	F	S
40						1	2
41	3	4	5	6	7	8	9
42	10	11	12	13	14	15	16
43	17	18	19	20	21	22	23
44	24	25	26	27	28	29	30
45	31						

NOVEMBER
WK	S	M	T	W	T	F	S
45		1	2	3	4	5	6
46	7	8	9	10	11	12	13
47	14	15	16	17	18	19	20
48	21	22	23	24	25	26	27
49	28	29	30				

DECEMBER
WK	S	M	T	W	T	F
49				1	2	3
50	5	6	7	8	9	10
51	12	13	14	15	16	17
52	19	20	21	22	23	24
53	26	27	28	29	30	31

2011

JANUARY
WK	S	M	T	W	T	F	S
1							1
2	2	3	4	5	6	7	8
3	9	10	11	12	13	14	15
4	16	17	18	19	20	21	22
5	23	24	25	26	27	28	29
6	30	31					

FEBRUARY
WK	S	M	T	W	T	F	S
6			1	2	3	4	5
7	6	7	8	9	10	11	12
8	13	14	15	16	17	18	19
9	20	21	22	23	24	25	26
10	27	28					

MARCH
WK	S	M	T	W	T	F	S
10			1	2	3	4	5
11	6	7	8	9	10	11	12
12	13	14	15	16	17	18	19
13	20	21	22	23	24	25	26
14	27	28	29	30	31		

APRIL
WK	S	M	T	W	T	F
14						1
15	3	4	5	6	7	8
16	10	11	12	13	14	15
17	17	18	19	20	21	22
18	24	25	26	27	28	29

MAY
WK	S	M	T	W	T	F	S
19	1	2	3	4	5	6	7
20	8	9	10	11	12	13	14
21	15	16	17	18	19	20	21
22	22	23	24	25	26	27	28
23	29	30	31				

JUNE
WK	S	M	T	W	T	F	S
23				1	2	3	4
24	5	6	7	8	9	10	11
25	12	13	14	15	16	17	18
26	19	20	21	22	23	24	25
27	26	27	28	29	30		

JULY
WK	S	M	T	W	T	F	S
27						1	2
28	3	4	5	6	7	8	9
29	10	11	12	13	14	15	16
30	17	18	19	20	21	22	23
31	24	25	26	27	28	29	30
32	31						

AUGUST
WK	S	M	T	W	T	F
32		1	2	3	4	5
33	7	8	9	10	11	12
34	14	15	16	17	18	19
35	21	22	23	24	25	26
36	28	29	30	31		

SEPTEMBER
WK	S	M	T	W	T	F	S
36					1	2	3
37	4	5	6	7	8	9	10
38	11	12	13	14	15	16	17
39	18	19	20	21	22	23	24
40	25	26	27	28	29	30	

OCTOBER
WK	S	M	T	W	T	F	S
40							1
41	2	3	4	5	6	7	8
42	9	10	11	12	13	14	15
43	16	17	18	19	20	21	22
44	23	24	25	26	27	28	29
45	30	31					

NOVEMBER
WK	S	M	T	W	T	F	S
45			1	2	3	4	5
46	6	7	8	9	10	11	12
47	13	14	15	16	17	18	19
48	20	21	22	23	24	25	26
49	27	28	29	30			

DECEMBER
WK	S	M	T	W	T	F
49					1	2
50	4	5	6	7	8	9
51	11	12	13	14	15	16
52	18	19	20	21	22	23
53	25	26	27	28	29	30

Days To Remember   *Year* _____

	Date	Event
Jan		
Feb		
Mar		
Apr		
May		
Jun		

Days To Remember   *Year*____

	Date	Event
Jul		
Aug		
Sep		
Oct		
Nov		
Dec		

Days To Remember

*Year*_____

Date	Event
Jan	
Feb	
Mar	
Apr	
May	
Jun	

Days To Remember   *Year*____

	Date	Event
Jul		
Aug		
Sep		
Oct		
Nov		
Dec		

Days To Remember

*Year*_____

Date		Event
Jan		
Feb		
Mar		
Apr		
May		
Jun		

Days To Remember

Year _____

Date	Event
Jul	
Aug	
Sep	
Oct	
Nov	
Dec	

Days To Remember   *Year*_____

Date	Event
Jul	
Aug	
Sep	
Oct	
Nov	
Dec	

Days To Remember   *Year*____

Date   Event

Jul	
Aug	
Sep	
Oct	
Nov	
Dec	

My Personal Index

Date   **Subject**

_____   _____

_____   _____

_____   _____

_____   _____

_____   _____

_____   _____

_____   _____

_____   _____

_____   _____

_____   _____

_____   _____

_____   _____

_____   _____

_____   _____

_____   _____

_____   _____

_____   _____

_____   _____

_____   _____

_____   _____

_____   _____

_____   _____

_____   _____

_____   _____

_____   _____

_____   _____

_____   _____

My Personal Index

Date   **Subject**

_____   _____

_____   _____

_____   _____

_____   _____

_____   _____

_____   _____

_____   _____

_____   _____

_____   _____

_____   _____

_____   _____

_____   _____

_____   _____

_____   _____

_____   _____

_____   _____

_____   _____

_____   _____

_____   _____

_____   _____

_____   _____

_____   _____

_____   _____

A wise man will hear and
increase learning,
And a man of understanding
will attain wise counsel.

Proverbs 1:5

Speaker: _____ Date: _____

Subject: _____ Place: _____

Main Scripture Texts: _____ _____

Old Testament References

Gen _____	2 Chr _____	Dan _____
Ex _____	Ezra _____	Hos _____
Lev _____	Neh _____	Joel _____
Num _____	Est _____	Amos _____
Dt _____	Job _____	Obad _____
Josh _____	Ps _____	Jon _____
Jud _____	Prov _____	Mic _____
Ruth _____	Eccl _____	Nah _____
1 Sam _____	Song _____	Hab _____
2 Sam _____	Isa _____	Zeph _____
1 Ki _____	Jer _____	Hag _____
2 Ki _____	Lam _____	Zech _____
1 Chr _____	Ezek _____	Mal _____

New Testament References

Mt _____	Eph _____	Heb _____
Mk _____	Phil _____	Jas _____
Lk _____	Col _____	1 Pet _____
Jn _____	1 Th _____	2 Pet _____
Acts _____	2 Th _____	1 Jn _____
Rom _____	1 Tim _____	2 Jn _____
1 Cor _____	2 Tim _____	3 Jn _____
2 Cor _____	Ti _____	Jude _____
Gal _____	Phile _____	Rev _____

"Study to shew thyself approved unto God, a workman that needeth not be ashamed, rightly dividing the word of truth" (II Tim 2:15).

Notes

Notes

Notes

Speaker: _____   Date: _____

Subject: _____   Place: _____

Main Scripture Texts: _____   _____

Old Testament References

Gen _____	2 Chr _____	Dan _____
Ex _____	Ezra _____	Hos _____
Lev _____	Neh _____	Joel _____
Num _____	Est _____	Amos_____
Dt _____	Job _____	Obad _____
Josh _____	Ps _____	Jon _____
Jud _____	Prov _____	Mic _____
Ruth _____	Eccl _____	Nah _____
1 Sam_____	Song _____	Hab _____
2 Sam_____	Isa _____	Zeph _____
1 Ki _____	Jer _____	Hag _____
2 Ki _____	Lam _____	Zech _____
1 Chr _____	Ezek _____	Mal _____

New Testament References

Mt _____	Eph _____	Heb _____
Mk _____	Phil _____	Jas _____
Lk _____	Col _____	1 Pet _____
Jn _____	1 Th _____	2 Pet _____
Acts _____	2 Th _____	1 Jn _____
Rom _____	1 Tim_____	2 Jn _____
1 Cor_____	2 Tim_____	3 Jn _____
2 Cor_____	Ti _____	Jude _____
Gal _____	Phile _____	Rev _____

"Study to shew thyself approved unto God, a workman that needeth not be ashamed, rightly dividing the word of truth" (II Tim 2:15).

<u>Notes</u>

Notes

Notes

Speaker: _____ Date: _____

Subject: _____ Place: _____

Main Scripture Texts: _____ _____

Old Testament References

Gen _____	2 Chr _____	Dan _____
Ex _____	Ezra _____	Hos _____
Lev _____	Neh _____	Joel _____
Num _____	Est _____	Amos _____
Dt _____	Job _____	Obad _____
Josh _____	Ps _____	Jon _____
Jud _____	Prov _____	Mic _____
Ruth _____	Eccl _____	Nah _____
1 Sam _____	Song _____	Hab _____
2 Sam _____	Isa _____	Zeph _____
1 Ki _____	Jer _____	Hag _____
2 Ki _____	Lam _____	Zech _____
1 Chr _____	Ezek _____	Mal _____

New Testament References

Mt _____	Eph _____	Heb _____
Mk _____	Phil _____	Jas _____
Lk _____	Col _____	1 Pet _____
Jn _____	1 Th _____	2 Pet _____
Acts _____	2 Th _____	1 Jn _____
Rom _____	1 Tim _____	2 Jn _____
1 Cor _____	2 Tim _____	3 Jn _____
2 Cor _____	Ti _____	Jude _____
Gal _____	Phile _____	Rev _____

"Study to shew thyself approved unto God, a workman that needeth not be ashamed, rightly dividing the word of truth" (II Tim 2:15).

Notes

<u>Notes</u>

<u>Notes</u>

Speaker: _____ Date: _____

Subject: _____ Place: _____

Main Scripture Texts: _____ _____

Old Testament References

Gen _____	2 Chr _____	Dan _____
Ex _____	Ezra _____	Hos _____
Lev _____	Neh _____	Joel _____
Num _____	Est _____	Amos _____
Dt _____	Job _____	Obad _____
Josh _____	Ps _____	Jon _____
Jud _____	Prov _____	Mic _____
Ruth _____	Eccl _____	Nah _____
1 Sam _____	Song _____	Hab _____
2 Sam _____	Isa _____	Zeph _____
1 Ki _____	Jer _____	Hag _____
2 Ki _____	Lam _____	Zech _____
1 Chr _____	Ezek _____	Mal _____

New Testament References

Mt _____	Eph _____	Heb _____
Mk _____	Phil _____	Jas _____
Lk _____	Col _____	1 Pet _____
Jn _____	1 Th _____	2 Pet _____
Acts _____	2 Th _____	1 Jn _____
Rom _____	1 Tim _____	2 Jn _____
1 Cor _____	2 Tim _____	3 Jn _____
2 Cor _____	Ti _____	Jude _____
Gal _____	Phile _____	Rev _____

"Study to shew thyself approved unto God, a workman that needeth not be ashamed, rightly dividing the word of truth" (II Tim 2:15).

Notes

Notes

Notes

Speaker: _____ Date: _____

Subject: _____ Place: _____

Main Scripture Texts: _____ _____

Old Testament References

Gen _____	2 Chr _____	Dan _____
Ex _____	Ezra _____	Hos _____
Lev _____	Neh _____	Joel _____
Num _____	Est _____	Amos _____
Dt _____	Job _____	Obad _____
Josh _____	Ps _____	Jon _____
Jud _____	Prov _____	Mic _____
Ruth _____	Eccl _____	Nah _____
1 Sam _____	Song _____	Hab _____
2 Sam _____	Isa _____	Zeph _____
1 Ki _____	Jer _____	Hag _____
2 Ki _____	Lam _____	Zech _____
1 Chr _____	Ezek _____	Mal _____

New Testament References

Mt _____	Eph _____	Heb _____
Mk _____	Phil _____	Jas _____
Lk _____	Col _____	1 Pet _____
Jn _____	1 Th _____	2 Pet _____
Acts _____	2 Th _____	1 Jn _____
Rom _____	1 Tim _____	2 Jn _____
1 Cor _____	2 Tim _____	3 Jn _____
2 Cor _____	Ti _____	Jude _____
Gal _____	Phile _____	Rev _____

"Study to shew thyself approved unto God, a workman that needeth not be ashamed, rightly dividing the word of truth" (II Tim 2:15).

Notes

Speaker: _____ Date: _____

Subject: _____ Place: _____

Main Scripture Texts: _____ _____

Old Testament References

Gen _____	2 Chr _____	Dan _____
Ex _____	Ezra _____	Hos _____
Lev _____	Neh _____	Joel _____
Num _____	Est _____	Amos_____
Dt _____	Job _____	Obad _____
Josh _____	Ps _____	Jon _____
Jud _____	Prov _____	Mic _____
Ruth _____	Eccl _____	Nah _____
1 Sam_____	Song _____	Hab _____
2 Sam_____	Isa _____	Zeph _____
1 Ki _____	Jer _____	Hag _____
2 Ki _____	Lam _____	Zech _____
1 Chr _____	Ezek _____	Mal _____

New Testament References

Mt _____	Eph _____	Heb _____
Mk _____	Phil _____	Jas _____
Lk _____	Col _____	1 Pet _____
Jn _____	1 Th _____	2 Pet _____
Acts _____	2 Th _____	1 Jn _____
Rom _____	1 Tim_____	2 Jn _____
1 Cor_____	2 Tim_____	3 Jn _____
2 Cor_____	Ti _____	Jude _____
Gal _____	Phile _____	Rev _____

"Study to shew thyself approved unto God, a workman that needeth not be ashamed, rightly dividing the word of truth" (II Tim 2:15).

Notes

<u>Notes</u>

Notes

Speaker: _____ Date: _____

Subject: _____ Place: _____

Main Scripture Texts: _____ _____

Old Testament References

Gen _____	2 Chr _____	Dan _____
Ex _____	Ezra _____	Hos _____
Lev _____	Neh _____	Joel _____
Num _____	Est _____	Amos _____
Dt _____	Job _____	Obad _____
Josh _____	Ps _____	Jon _____
Jud _____	Prov _____	Mic _____
Ruth _____	Eccl _____	Nah _____
1 Sam _____	Song _____	Hab _____
2 Sam _____	Isa _____	Zeph _____
1 Ki _____	Jer _____	Hag _____
2 Ki _____	Lam _____	Zech _____
1 Chr _____	Ezek _____	Mal _____

New Testament References

Mt _____	Eph _____	Heb _____
Mk _____	Phil _____	Jas _____
Lk _____	Col _____	1 Pet _____
Jn _____	1 Th _____	2 Pet _____
Acts _____	2 Th _____	1 Jn _____
Rom _____	1 Tim _____	2 Jn _____
1 Cor _____	2 Tim _____	3 Jn _____
2 Cor _____	Ti _____	Jude _____
Gal _____	Phile _____	Rev _____

"Study to shew thyself approved unto God, a workman that needeth not be ashamed, rightly dividing the word of truth" (II Tim 2:15).

Notes

Notes

Notes

Speaker: _____ Date: _____

Subject: _____ Place: _____

Main Scripture Texts: _____ _____

Old Testament References

Gen _____	2 Chr _____	Dan _____
Ex _____	Ezra _____	Hos _____
Lev _____	Neh _____	Joel _____
Num _____	Est _____	Amos _____
Dt _____	Job _____	Obad _____
Josh _____	Ps _____	Jon _____
Jud _____	Prov _____	Mic _____
Ruth _____	Eccl _____	Nah _____
1 Sam _____	Song _____	Hab _____
2 Sam _____	Isa _____	Zeph _____
1 Ki _____	Jer _____	Hag _____
2 Ki _____	Lam _____	Zech _____
1 Chr _____	Ezek _____	Mal _____

New Testament References

Mt _____	Eph _____	Heb _____
Mk _____	Phil _____	Jas _____
Lk _____	Col _____	1 Pet _____
Jn _____	1 Th _____	2 Pet _____
Acts _____	2 Th _____	1 Jn _____
Rom _____	1 Tim _____	2 Jn _____
1 Cor _____	2 Tim _____	3 Jn _____
2 Cor _____	Ti _____	Jude _____
Gal _____	Phile _____	Rev _____

"Study to shew thyself approved unto God, a workman that needeth not be ashamed, rightly dividing the word of truth" (II Tim 2:15).

Notes

Notes

Notes

Speaker: _____ Date: _____

Subject: _____ Place:_____

Main Scripture Texts: _____ _____

Old Testament References

Gen _____	2 Chr _____	Dan _____
Ex _____	Ezra _____	Hos _____
Lev _____	Neh _____	Joel _____
Num _____	Est _____	Amos_____
Dt _____	Job _____	Obad _____
Josh _____	Ps _____	Jon _____
Jud _____	Prov _____	Mic _____
Ruth _____	Eccl _____	Nah _____
1 Sam_____	Song _____	Hab _____
2 Sam_____	Isa _____	Zeph _____
1 Ki _____	Jer _____	Hag _____
2 Ki _____	Lam _____	Zech _____
1 Chr _____	Ezek _____	Mal _____

New Testament References

Mt _____	Eph _____	Heb _____
Mk _____	Phil _____	Jas _____
Lk _____	Col _____	1 Pet _____
Jn _____	1 Th _____	2 Pet _____
Acts _____	2 Th _____	1 Jn _____
Rom _____	1 Tim_____	2 Jn _____
1 Cor_____	2 Tim_____	3 Jn _____
2 Cor_____	Ti _____	Jude _____
Gal _____	Phile _____	Rev _____

"Study to shew thyself approved unto God, a workman that needeth not be ashamed, rightly dividing the word of truth" (II Tim 2:15).

Notes

Notes

Notes

Speaker: _____ Date: _____

Subject: _____ Place:_____

Main Scripture Texts: _____ _____

Old Testament References

Gen _____	2 Chr_____	Dan _____
Ex _____	Ezra _____	Hos _____
Lev _____	Neh _____	Joel _____
Num _____	Est _____	Amos_____
Dt _____	Job _____	Obad _____
Josh _____	Ps _____	Jon _____
Jud _____	Prov _____	Mic _____
Ruth _____	Eccl _____	Nah _____
1 Sam_____	Song _____	Hab _____
2 Sam_____	Isa _____	Zeph _____
1 Ki _____	Jer _____	Hag _____
2 Ki _____	Lam _____	Zech _____
1 Chr_____	Ezek _____	Mal _____

New Testament References

Mt _____	Eph _____	Heb _____
Mk _____	Phil _____	Jas _____
Lk _____	Col _____	1 Pet _____
Jn _____	1 Th _____	2 Pet _____
Acts _____	2 Th _____	1 Jn _____
Rom _____	1 Tim_____	2 Jn _____
1 Cor_____	2 Tim_____	3 Jn _____
2 Cor_____	Ti _____	Jude _____
Gal _____	Phile _____	Rev _____

"Study to shew thyself approved unto God, a workman that needeth not be ashamed, rightly dividing the word of truth" (II Tim 2:15).

Notes

Notes

Notes

Speaker: _____ Date: _____

Subject: _____ Place: _____

Main Scripture Texts: _____ _____

Old Testament References

Gen _____	2 Chr _____	Dan _____
Ex _____	Ezra _____	Hos _____
Lev _____	Neh _____	Joel _____
Num _____	Est _____	Amos_____
Dt _____	Job _____	Obad _____
Josh _____	Ps _____	Jon _____
Jud _____	Prov _____	Mic _____
Ruth _____	Eccl _____	Nah _____
1 Sam_____	Song _____	Hab _____
2 Sam_____	Isa _____	Zeph _____
1 Ki _____	Jer _____	Hag _____
2 Ki _____	Lam _____	Zech _____
1 Chr _____	Ezek _____	Mal _____

New Testament References

Mt _____	Eph _____	Heb _____
Mk _____	Phil _____	Jas _____
Lk _____	Col _____	1 Pet _____
Jn _____	1 Th _____	2 Pet _____
Acts _____	2 Th _____	1 Jn _____
Rom _____	1 Tim_____	2 Jn _____
1 Cor_____	2 Tim_____	3 Jn _____
2 Cor_____	Ti _____	Jude _____
Gal _____	Phile _____	Rev _____

"Study to shew thyself approved unto God, a workman that needeth not be ashamed, rightly dividing the word of truth" (II Tim 2:15).

Notes

<u>Notes</u>

Notes

Speaker: _____ Date: _____

Subject: _____ Place:_____

Main Scripture Texts: _____ _____

Old Testament References

Gen _____	2 Chr_____	Dan _____
Ex _____	Ezra _____	Hos _____
Lev _____	Neh _____	Joel _____
Num _____	Est _____	Amos_____
Dt _____	Job _____	Obad _____
Josh _____	Ps _____	Jon _____
Jud _____	Prov _____	Mic _____
Ruth _____	Eccl _____	Nah _____
1 Sam_____	Song _____	Hab _____
2 Sam_____	Isa _____	Zeph _____
1 Ki _____	Jer _____	Hag _____
2 Ki _____	Lam _____	Zech _____
1 Chr_____	Ezek _____	Mal _____

New Testament References

Mt _____	Eph _____	Heb _____
Mk _____	Phil _____	Jas _____
Lk _____	Col _____	1 Pet _____
Jn _____	1 Th _____	2 Pet _____
Acts _____	2 Th _____	1 Jn _____
Rom _____	1 Tim_____	2 Jn _____
1 Cor_____	2 Tim_____	3 Jn _____
2 Cor_____	Ti _____	Jude _____
Gal _____	Phile _____	Rev _____

"Study to shew thyself approved unto God, a workman that needeth not be ashamed, rightly dividing the word of truth" (II Tim 2:15).

Notes

Notes

Notes

Speaker: _____ Date: _____

Subject: _____ Place: _____

Main Scripture Texts: _____ _____

Old Testament References

Gen _____	2 Chr _____	Dan _____
Ex _____	Ezra _____	Hos _____
Lev _____	Neh _____	Joel _____
Num _____	Est _____	Amos_____
Dt _____	Job _____	Obad _____
Josh _____	Ps _____	Jon _____
Jud _____	Prov _____	Mic _____
Ruth _____	Eccl _____	Nah _____
1 Sam_____	Song _____	Hab _____
2 Sam_____	Isa _____	Zeph _____
1 Ki _____	Jer _____	Hag _____
2 Ki _____	Lam _____	Zech _____
1 Chr _____	Ezek _____	Mal _____

New Testament References

Mt _____	Eph _____	Heb _____
Mk _____	Phil _____	Jas _____
Lk _____	Col _____	1 Pet _____
Jn _____	1 Th _____	2 Pet _____
Acts _____	2 Th _____	1 Jn _____
Rom _____	1 Tim_____	2 Jn _____
1 Cor_____	2 Tim_____	3 Jn _____
2 Cor_____	Ti _____	Jude _____
Gal _____	Phile _____	Rev _____

"Study to shew thyself approved unto God, a workman that needeth not be ashamed, rightly dividing the word of truth" (II Tim 2:15).

Notes

Notes

Notes

Speaker: _____ Date: _____

Subject: _____ Place: _____

Main Scripture Texts: _____ _____

Old Testament References

Gen	_____	2 Chr	_____	Dan	_____
Ex	_____	Ezra	_____	Hos	_____
Lev	_____	Neh	_____	Joel	_____
Num	_____	Est	_____	Amos	_____
Dt	_____	Job	_____	Obad	_____
Josh	_____	Ps	_____	Jon	_____
Jud	_____	Prov	_____	Mic	_____
Ruth	_____	Eccl	_____	Nah	_____
1 Sam	_____	Song	_____	Hab	_____
2 Sam	_____	Isa	_____	Zeph	_____
1 Ki	_____	Jer	_____	Hag	_____
2 Ki	_____	Lam	_____	Zech	_____
1 Chr	_____	Ezek	_____	Mal	_____

New Testament References

Mt	_____	Eph	_____	Heb	_____
Mk	_____	Phil	_____	Jas	_____
Lk	_____	Col	_____	1 Pet	_____
Jn	_____	1 Th	_____	2 Pet	_____
Acts	_____	2 Th	_____	1 Jn	_____
Rom	_____	1 Tim	_____	2 Jn	_____
1 Cor	_____	2 Tim	_____	3 Jn	_____
2 Cor	_____	Ti	_____	Jude	_____
Gal	_____	Phile	_____	Rev	_____

"Study to shew thyself approved unto God, a workman that needeth not be ashamed, rightly dividing the word of truth" (II Tim 2:15).

Notes

<u>Notes</u>

<u>Notes</u>

Speaker: _____ Date: _____

Subject: _____ Place: _____

Main Scripture Texts: _____ _____

Old Testament References

Gen	_____	2 Chr	_____	Dan	_____
Ex	_____	Ezra	_____	Hos	_____
Lev	_____	Neh	_____	Joel	_____
Num	_____	Est	_____	Amos	_____
Dt	_____	Job	_____	Obad	_____
Josh	_____	Ps	_____	Jon	_____
Jud	_____	Prov	_____	Mic	_____
Ruth	_____	Eccl	_____	Nah	_____
1 Sam	_____	Song	_____	Hab	_____
2 Sam	_____	Isa	_____	Zeph	_____
1 Ki	_____	Jer	_____	Hag	_____
2 Ki	_____	Lam	_____	Zech	_____
1 Chr	_____	Ezek	_____	Mal	_____

New Testament References

Mt	_____	Eph	_____	Heb	_____
Mk	_____	Phil	_____	Jas	_____
Lk	_____	Col	_____	1 Pet	_____
Jn	_____	1 Th	_____	2 Pet	_____
Acts	_____	2 Th	_____	1 Jn	_____
Rom	_____	1 Tim	_____	2 Jn	_____
1 Cor	_____	2 Tim	_____	3 Jn	_____
2 Cor	_____	Ti	_____	Jude	_____
Gal	_____	Phile	_____	Rev	_____

"Study to shew thyself approved unto God, a workman that needeth not be ashamed, rightly dividing the word of truth" (II Tim 2:15).

Notes

Notes

Notes

Speaker: _____ Date: _____

Subject: _____ Place: _____

Main Scripture Texts: _____ _____

Old Testament References

Gen	_____	2 Chr	_____	Dan	_____
Ex	_____	Ezra	_____	Hos	_____
Lev	_____	Neh	_____	Joel	_____
Num	_____	Est	_____	Amos	_____
Dt	_____	Job	_____	Obad	_____
Josh	_____	Ps	_____	Jon	_____
Jud	_____	Prov	_____	Mic	_____
Ruth	_____	Eccl	_____	Nah	_____
1 Sam	_____	Song	_____	Hab	_____
2 Sam	_____	Isa	_____	Zeph	_____
1 Ki	_____	Jer	_____	Hag	_____
2 Ki	_____	Lam	_____	Zech	_____
1 Chr	_____	Ezek	_____	Mal	_____

New Testament References

Mt	_____	Eph	_____	Heb	_____
Mk	_____	Phil	_____	Jas	_____
Lk	_____	Col	_____	1 Pet	_____
Jn	_____	1 Th	_____	2 Pet	_____
Acts	_____	2 Th	_____	1 Jn	_____
Rom	_____	1 Tim	_____	2 Jn	_____
1 Cor	_____	2 Tim	_____	3 Jn	_____
2 Cor	_____	Ti	_____	Jude	_____
Gal	_____	Phile	_____	Rev	_____

"Study to shew thyself approved unto God, a workman that needeth not be ashamed, rightly dividing the word of truth" (II Tim 2:15).

Notes

<u>Notes</u>

Notes

Speaker: _____ Date: _____

Subject: _____ Place: _____

Main Scripture Texts: _____ _____

Old Testament References

Gen _____	2 Chr _____	Dan _____
Ex _____	Ezra _____	Hos _____
Lev _____	Neh _____	Joel _____
Num _____	Est _____	Amos _____
Dt _____	Job _____	Obad _____
Josh _____	Ps _____	Jon _____
Jud _____	Prov _____	Mic _____
Ruth _____	Eccl _____	Nah _____
1 Sam _____	Song _____	Hab _____
2 Sam _____	Isa _____	Zeph _____
1 Ki _____	Jer _____	Hag _____
2 Ki _____	Lam _____	Zech _____
1 Chr _____	Ezek _____	Mal _____

New Testament References

Mt _____	Eph _____	Heb _____
Mk _____	Phil _____	Jas _____
Lk _____	Col _____	1 Pet _____
Jn _____	1 Th _____	2 Pet _____
Acts _____	2 Th _____	1 Jn _____
Rom _____	1 Tim _____	2 Jn _____
1 Cor _____	2 Tim _____	3 Jn _____
2 Cor _____	Ti _____	Jude _____
Gal _____	Phile _____	Rev _____

"Study to shew thyself approved unto God, a workman that needeth not be ashamed, rightly dividing the word of truth" (II Tim 2:15).

Notes

<u>Notes</u>

Notes

Speaker: _____   Date: _____

Subject: _____   Place:_____

Main Scripture Texts: _____   _____

Old Testament References

Gen _____	2 Chr _____	Dan _____
Ex _____	Ezra _____	Hos _____
Lev _____	Neh _____	Joel _____
Num _____	Est _____	Amos_____
Dt _____	Job _____	Obad _____
Josh _____	Ps _____	Jon _____
Jud _____	Prov _____	Mic _____
Ruth _____	Eccl _____	Nah _____
1 Sam_____	Song _____	Hab _____
2 Sam_____	Isa _____	Zeph _____
1 Ki _____	Jer _____	Hag _____
2 Ki _____	Lam _____	Zech _____
1 Chr _____	Ezek _____	Mal _____

New Testament References

Mt _____	Eph _____	Heb _____
Mk _____	Phil _____	Jas _____
Lk _____	Col _____	1 Pet _____
Jn _____	1 Th _____	2 Pet _____
Acts _____	2 Th _____	1 Jn _____
Rom _____	1 Tim_____	2 Jn _____
1 Cor_____	2 Tim_____	3 Jn _____
2 Cor_____	Ti _____	Jude _____
Gal _____	Phile _____	Rev _____

"Study to shew thyself approved unto God, a workman that needeth not be ashamed, rightly dividing the word of truth" (II Tim 2:15).

Notes

Notes

Notes

Speaker: _____   Date: _____

Subject: _____   Place: _____

Main Scripture Texts: _____   _____

Old Testament References

Gen _____	2 Chr _____	Dan _____
Ex _____	Ezra _____	Hos _____
Lev _____	Neh _____	Joel _____
Num _____	Est _____	Amos _____
Dt _____	Job _____	Obad _____
Josh _____	Ps _____	Jon _____
Jud _____	Prov _____	Mic _____
Ruth _____	Eccl _____	Nah _____
1 Sam _____	Song _____	Hab _____
2 Sam _____	Isa _____	Zeph _____
1 Ki _____	Jer _____	Hag _____
2 Ki _____	Lam _____	Zech _____
1 Chr _____	Ezek _____	Mal _____

New Testament References

Mt _____	Eph _____	Heb _____
Mk _____	Phil _____	Jas _____
Lk _____	Col _____	1 Pet _____
Jn _____	1 Th _____	2 Pet _____
Acts _____	2 Th _____	1 Jn _____
Rom _____	1 Tim _____	2 Jn _____
1 Cor _____	2 Tim _____	3 Jn _____
2 Cor _____	Ti _____	Jude _____
Gal _____	Phile _____	Rev _____

"Study to shew thyself approved unto God, a workman that needeth not be ashamed, rightly dividing the word of truth" (II Tim 2:15).

Notes

<u>Notes</u>

Notes

Speaker: _____ Date: _____

Subject: _____ _____ Place:_____

Main Scripture Texts: _____ _____

Old Testament References

Gen _____	2 Chr _____	Dan _____
Ex _____	Ezra _____	Hos _____
Lev _____	Neh _____	Joel _____
Num _____	Est _____	Amos_____
Dt _____	Job _____	Obad _____
Josh _____	Ps _____	Jon _____
Jud _____	Prov _____	Mic _____
Ruth _____	Eccl _____	Nah _____
1 Sam_____	Song _____	Hab _____
2 Sam_____	Isa _____	Zeph _____
1 Ki _____	Jer _____	Hag _____
2 Ki _____	Lam _____	Zech _____
1 Chr _____	Ezek _____	Mal _____

New Testament References

Mt _____	Eph _____	Heb _____
Mk _____	Phil _____	Jas _____
Lk _____	Col _____	1 Pet _____
Jn _____	1 Th _____	2 Pet _____
Acts _____	2 Th _____	1 Jn _____
Rom _____	1 Tim_____	2 Jn _____
1 Cor _____	2 Tim_____	3 Jn _____
2 Cor _____	Ti _____	Jude _____
Gal _____	Phile _____	Rev _____

"Study to shew thyself approved unto God, a workman that needeth not be ashamed, rightly dividing the word of truth" (II Tim 2:15).

Notes

Notes

<u>Notes</u>

Speaker: _____ Date: _____

Subject: _____ Place:_____

Main Scripture Texts: _____ _____

Old Testament References

Gen _____	2 Chr _____	Dan _____
Ex _____	Ezra _____	Hos _____
Lev _____	Neh _____	Joel _____
Num _____	Est _____	Amos_____
Dt _____	Job _____	Obad _____
Josh _____	Ps _____	Jon _____
Jud _____	Prov _____	Mic _____
Ruth _____	Eccl _____	Nah _____
1 Sam_____	Song _____	Hab _____
2 Sam_____	Isa _____	Zeph _____
1 Ki _____	Jer _____	Hag _____
2 Ki _____	Lam _____	Zech _____
1 Chr_____	Ezek _____	Mal _____

New Testament References

Mt _____	Eph _____	Heb _____
Mk _____	Phil _____	Jas _____
Lk _____	Col _____	1 Pet _____
Jn _____	1 Th _____	2 Pet _____
Acts _____	2 Th _____	1 Jn _____
Rom _____	1 Tim_____	2 Jn _____
1 Cor_____	2 Tim_____	3 Jn _____
2 Cor_____	Ti _____	Jude _____
Gal _____	Phile _____	Rev _____

"Study to shew thyself approved unto God, a workman that needeth not be ashamed, rightly dividing the word of truth" (II Tim 2:15).

Notes

Notes

Notes

Speaker: _____ Date: _____

Subject: _____ Place: _____

Main Scripture Texts: _____ _____

Old Testament References

Gen	_____	2 Chr	_____	Dan	_____
Ex	_____	Ezra	_____	Hos	_____
Lev	_____	Neh	_____	Joel	_____
Num	_____	Est	_____	Amos	_____
Dt	_____	Job	_____	Obad	_____
Josh	_____	Ps	_____	Jon	_____
Jud	_____	Prov	_____	Mic	_____
Ruth	_____	Eccl	_____	Nah	_____
1 Sam	_____	Song	_____	Hab	_____
2 Sam	_____	Isa	_____	Zeph	_____
1 Ki	_____	Jer	_____	Hag	_____
2 Ki	_____	Lam	_____	Zech	_____
1 Chr	_____	Ezek	_____	Mal	_____

New Testament References

Mt	_____	Eph	_____	Heb	_____
Mk	_____	Phil	_____	Jas	_____
Lk	_____	Col	_____	1 Pet	_____
Jn	_____	1 Th	_____	2 Pet	_____
Acts	_____	2 Th	_____	1 Jn	_____
Rom	_____	1 Tim	_____	2 Jn	_____
1 Cor	_____	2 Tim	_____	3 Jn	_____
2 Cor	_____	Ti	_____	Jude	_____
Gal	_____	Phile	_____	Rev	_____

"Study to shew thyself approved unto God, a workman that needeth not be ashamed, rightly dividing the word of truth" (II Tim 2:15).

Notes

Notes

Notes

Speaker: _____ Date: _____

Subject: _____ Place:_____

Main Scripture Texts: _____ _____

Old Testament References

Gen _____	2 Chr _____	Dan _____
Ex _____	Ezra _____	Hos _____
Lev _____	Neh _____	Joel _____
Num _____	Est _____	Amos_____
Dt _____	Job _____	Obad _____
Josh _____	Ps _____	Jon _____
Jud _____	Prov _____	Mic _____
Ruth _____	Eccl _____	Nah _____
1 Sam_____	Song _____	Hab _____
2 Sam_____	Isa _____	Zeph _____
1 Ki _____	Jer _____	Hag _____
2 Ki _____	Lam _____	Zech _____
1 Chr _____	Ezek _____	Mal _____

New Testament References

Mt _____	Eph _____	Heb _____
Mk _____	Phil _____	Jas _____
Lk _____	Col _____	1 Pet _____
Jn _____	1 Th _____	2 Pet _____
Acts _____	2 Th _____	1 Jn _____
Rom _____	1 Tim_____	2 Jn _____
1 Cor_____	2 Tim_____	3 Jn _____
2 Cor_____	Ti _____	Jude _____
Gal _____	Phile _____	Rev _____

"Study to shew thyself approved unto God, a workman that needeth not be ashamed, rightly dividing the word of truth" (II Tim 2:15).

Notes

Notes

Notes

Speaker: _____ Date: _____

Subject: _____ Place: _____

Main Scripture Texts: _____ _____

Old Testament References

Gen _____	2 Chr _____	Dan _____
Ex _____	Ezra _____	Hos _____
Lev _____	Neh _____	Joel _____
Num _____	Est _____	Amos _____
Dt _____	Job _____	Obad _____
Josh _____	Ps _____	Jon _____
Jud _____	Prov _____	Mic _____
Ruth _____	Eccl _____	Nah _____
1 Sam _____	Song _____	Hab _____
2 Sam _____	Isa _____	Zeph _____
1 Ki _____	Jer _____	Hag _____
2 Ki _____	Lam _____	Zech _____
1 Chr _____	Ezek _____	Mal _____

New Testament References

Mt _____	Eph _____	Heb _____
Mk _____	Phil _____	Jas _____
Lk _____	Col _____	1 Pet _____
Jn _____	1 Th _____	2 Pet _____
Acts _____	2 Th _____	1 Jn _____
Rom _____	1 Tim _____	2 Jn _____
1 Cor _____	2 Tim _____	3 Jn _____
2 Cor _____	Ti _____	Jude _____
Gal _____	Phile _____	Rev _____

"Study to shew thyself approved unto God, a workman that needeth not be ashamed, rightly dividing the word of truth" (II Tim 2:15).

Notes

Notes

Notes

Speaker: _____ Date: _____

Subject: _____ Place: _____

Main Scripture Texts: _____ _____

Old Testament References

Gen _____	2 Chr _____	Dan _____
Ex _____	Ezra _____	Hos _____
Lev _____	Neh _____	Joel _____
Num _____	Est _____	Amos _____
Dt _____	Job _____	Obad _____
Josh _____	Ps _____	Jon _____
Jud _____	Prov _____	Mic _____
Ruth _____	Eccl _____	Nah _____
1 Sam _____	Song _____	Hab _____
2 Sam _____	Isa _____	Zeph _____
1 Ki _____	Jer _____	Hag _____
2 Ki _____	Lam _____	Zech _____
1 Chr _____	Ezek _____	Mal _____

New Testament References

Mt _____	Eph _____	Heb _____
Mk _____	Phil _____	Jas _____
Lk _____	Col _____	1 Pet _____
Jn _____	1 Th _____	2 Pet _____
Acts _____	2 Th _____	1 Jn _____
Rom _____	1 Tim _____	2 Jn _____
1 Cor _____	2 Tim _____	3 Jn _____
2 Cor _____	Ti _____	Jude _____
Gal _____	Phile _____	Rev _____

"Study to shew thyself approved unto God, a workman that needeth not be ashamed, rightly dividing the word of truth" (II Tim 2:15).

Notes

Notes

Notes

Speaker: _____ Date: _____

Subject: _____ Place:_____

Main Scripture Texts: _____ _____

Old Testament References

Gen	_____	2 Chr	_____	Dan	_____
Ex	_____	Ezra	_____	Hos	_____
Lev	_____	Neh	_____	Joel	_____
Num	_____	Est	_____	Amos	_____
Dt	_____	Job	_____	Obad	_____
Josh	_____	Ps	_____	Jon	_____
Jud	_____	Prov	_____	Mic	_____
Ruth	_____	Eccl	_____	Nah	_____
1 Sam	_____	Song	_____	Hab	_____
2 Sam	_____	Isa	_____	Zeph	_____
1 Ki	_____	Jer	_____	Hag	_____
2 Ki	_____	Lam	_____	Zech	_____
1 Chr	_____	Ezek	_____	Mal	_____

New Testament References

Mt	_____	Eph	_____	Heb	_____
Mk	_____	Phil	_____	Jas	_____
Lk	_____	Col	_____	1 Pet	_____
Jn	_____	1 Th	_____	2 Pet	_____
Acts	_____	2 Th	_____	1 Jn	_____
Rom	_____	1 Tim	_____	2 Jn	_____
1 Cor	_____	2 Tim	_____	3 Jn	_____
2 Cor	_____	Ti	_____	Jude	_____
Gal	_____	Phile	_____	Rev	_____

"Study to shew thyself approved unto God, a workman that needeth not be ashamed, rightly dividing the word of truth" (II Tim 2:15).

Notes

Notes

Notes

Speaker: _____ Date: _____

Subject: _____ Place: _____

Main Scripture Texts: _____ _____

Old Testament References

Gen _____	2 Chr _____	Dan _____
Ex _____	Ezra _____	Hos _____
Lev _____	Neh _____	Joel _____
Num _____	Est _____	Amos _____
Dt _____	Job _____	Obad _____
Josh _____	Ps _____	Jon _____
Jud _____	Prov _____	Mic _____
Ruth _____	Eccl _____	Nah _____
1 Sam _____	Song _____	Hab _____
2 Sam _____	Isa _____	Zeph _____
1 Ki _____	Jer _____	Hag _____
2 Ki _____	Lam _____	Zech _____
1 Chr _____	Ezek _____	Mal _____

New Testament References

Mt _____	Eph _____	Heb _____
Mk _____	Phil _____	Jas _____
Lk _____	Col _____	1 Pet _____
Jn _____	1 Th _____	2 Pet _____
Acts _____	2 Th _____	1 Jn _____
Rom _____	1 Tim _____	2 Jn _____
1 Cor _____	2 Tim _____	3 Jn _____
2 Cor _____	Ti _____	Jude _____
Gal _____	Phile _____	Rev _____

"Study to shew thyself approved unto God, a workman that needeth not be ashamed, rightly dividing the word of truth" (II Tim 2:15).

Notes

Notes

Notes

Speaker: _____ Date: _____

Subject: _____ Place: _____

Main Scripture Texts: _____ _____

Old Testament References

Gen _____	2 Chr _____	Dan _____
Ex _____	Ezra _____	Hos _____
Lev _____	Neh _____	Joel _____
Num _____	Est _____	Amos _____
Dt _____	Job _____	Obad _____
Josh _____	Ps _____	Jon _____
Jud _____	Prov _____	Mic _____
Ruth _____	Eccl _____	Nah _____
1 Sam _____	Song _____	Hab _____
2 Sam _____	Isa _____	Zeph _____
1 Ki _____	Jer _____	Hag _____
2 Ki _____	Lam _____	Zech _____
1 Chr _____	Ezek _____	Mal _____

New Testament References

Mt _____	Eph _____	Heb _____
Mk _____	Phil _____	Jas _____
Lk _____	Col _____	1 Pet _____
Jn _____	1 Th _____	2 Pet _____
Acts _____	2 Th _____	1 Jn _____
Rom _____	1 Tim _____	2 Jn _____
1 Cor _____	2 Tim _____	3 Jn _____
2 Cor _____	Ti _____	Jude _____
Gal _____	Phile _____	Rev _____

"Study to shew thyself approved unto God, a workman that needeth not be ashamed, rightly dividing the word of truth" (II Tim 2:15).

Notes

Notes

Notes

Speaker: _____ Date: _____

Subject: _____ Place: _____

Main Scripture Texts: _____ _____

Old Testament References

Gen _____	2 Chr _____	Dan _____
Ex _____	Ezra _____	Hos _____
Lev _____	Neh _____	Joel _____
Num _____	Est _____	Amos _____
Dt _____	Job _____	Obad _____
Josh _____	Ps _____	Jon _____
Jud _____	Prov _____	Mic _____
Ruth _____	Eccl _____	Nah _____
1 Sam _____	Song _____	Hab _____
2 Sam _____	Isa _____	Zeph _____
1 Ki _____	Jer _____	Hag _____
2 Ki _____	Lam _____	Zech _____
1 Chr _____	Ezek _____	Mal _____

New Testament References

Mt _____	Eph _____	Heb _____
Mk _____	Phil _____	Jas _____
Lk _____	Col _____	1 Pet _____
Jn _____	1 Th _____	2 Pet _____
Acts _____	2 Th _____	1 Jn _____
Rom _____	1 Tim _____	2 Jn _____
1 Cor _____	2 Tim _____	3 Jn _____
2 Cor _____	Ti _____	Jude _____
Gal _____	Phile _____	Rev _____

"Study to shew thyself approved unto God, a workman that needeth not be ashamed, rightly dividing the word of truth" (II Tim 2:15).

Notes

Notes

Notes

Speaker: _____ Date: _____

Subject: _____ Place: _____

Main Scripture Texts: _____ _____

Old Testament References

Gen _____	2 Chr _____	Dan _____
Ex _____	Ezra _____	Hos _____
Lev _____	Neh _____	Joel _____
Num _____	Est _____	Amos _____
Dt _____	Job _____	Obad _____
Josh _____	Ps _____	Jon _____
Jud _____	Prov _____	Mic _____
Ruth _____	Eccl _____	Nah _____
1 Sam _____	Song _____	Hab _____
2 Sam _____	Isa _____	Zeph _____
1 Ki _____	Jer _____	Hag _____
2 Ki _____	Lam _____	Zech _____
1 Chr _____	Ezek _____	Mal _____

New Testament References

Mt _____	Eph _____	Heb _____
Mk _____	Phil _____	Jas _____
Lk _____	Col _____	1 Pet _____
Jn _____	1 Th _____	2 Pet _____
Acts _____	2 Th _____	1 Jn _____
Rom _____	1 Tim _____	2 Jn _____
1 Cor _____	2 Tim _____	3 Jn _____
2 Cor _____	Ti _____	Jude _____
Gal _____	Phile _____	Rev _____

"Study to shew thyself approved unto God, a workman that needeth not be ashamed, rightly dividing the word of truth" (II Tim 2:15).

Notes

Notes

Notes

Speaker: _____ Date: _____

Subject: _____ Place:_____

Main Scripture Texts: _____ _____

Old Testament References

Gen _____	2 Chr _____	Dan _____
Ex _____	Ezra _____	Hos _____
Lev _____	Neh _____	Joel _____
Num _____	Est _____	Amos_____
Dt _____	Job _____	Obad _____
Josh _____	Ps _____	Jon _____
Jud _____	Prov _____	Mic _____
Ruth _____	Eccl _____	Nah _____
1 Sam_____	Song _____	Hab _____
2 Sam_____	Isa _____	Zeph _____
1 Ki _____	Jer _____	Hag _____
2 Ki _____	Lam _____	Zech _____
1 Chr _____	Ezek _____	Mal _____

New Testament References

Mt _____	Eph _____	Heb _____
Mk _____	Phil _____	Jas _____
Lk _____	Col _____	1 Pet _____
Jn _____	1 Th _____	2 Pet _____
Acts _____	2 Th _____	1 Jn _____
Rom _____	1 Tim_____	2 Jn _____
1 Cor_____	2 Tim_____	3 Jn _____
2 Cor_____	Ti _____	Jude _____
Gal _____	Phile _____	Rev _____

"Study to shew thyself approved unto God, a workman that needeth not be ashamed, rightly dividing the word of truth" (II Tim 2:15).

Notes

Notes

Notes

Speaker: _____   Date: _____

Subject: _____   Place: _____

Main Scripture Texts: _____   _____

Old Testament References

Gen _____	2 Chr _____	Dan _____
Ex _____	Ezra _____	Hos _____
Lev _____	Neh _____	Joel _____
Num _____	Est _____	Amos _____
Dt _____	Job _____	Obad _____
Josh _____	Ps _____	Jon _____
Jud _____	Prov _____	Mic _____
Ruth _____	Eccl _____	Nah _____
1 Sam _____	Song _____	Hab _____
2 Sam _____	Isa _____	Zeph _____
1 Ki _____	Jer _____	Hag _____
2 Ki _____	Lam _____	Zech _____
1 Chr _____	Ezek _____	Mal _____

New Testament References

Mt _____	Eph _____	Heb _____
Mk _____	Phil _____	Jas _____
Lk _____	Col _____	1 Pet _____
Jn _____	1 Th _____	2 Pet _____
Acts _____	2 Th _____	1 Jn _____
Rom _____	1 Tim _____	2 Jn _____
1 Cor _____	2 Tim _____	3 Jn _____
2 Cor _____	Ti _____	Jude _____
Gal _____	Phile _____	Rev _____

"Study to shew thyself approved unto God, a workman that needeth not be ashamed, rightly dividing the word of truth" (II Tim 2:15).

Notes

Notes

Notes

Speaker: _____ Date: _____

Subject: _____ Place:_____

Main Scripture Texts: _____ _____

Old Testament References

Gen _____	2 Chr _____	Dan _____
Ex _____	Ezra _____	Hos _____
Lev _____	Neh _____	Joel _____
Num _____	Est _____	Amos _____
Dt _____	Job _____	Obad _____
Josh _____	Ps _____	Jon _____
Jud _____	Prov _____	Mic _____
Ruth _____	Eccl _____	Nah _____
1 Sam _____	Song _____	Hab _____
2 Sam _____	Isa _____	Zeph _____
1 Ki _____	Jer _____	Hag _____
2 Ki _____	Lam _____	Zech _____
1 Chr _____	Ezek _____	Mal _____

New Testament References

Mt _____	Eph _____	Heb _____
Mk _____	Phil _____	Jas _____
Lk _____	Col _____	1 Pet _____
Jn _____	1 Th _____	2 Pet _____
Acts _____	2 Th _____	1 Jn _____
Rom _____	1 Tim _____	2 Jn _____
1 Cor _____	2 Tim _____	3 Jn _____
2 Cor _____	Ti _____	Jude _____
Gal _____	Phile _____	Rev _____

"Study to shew thyself approved unto God, a workman that needeth not be ashamed, rightly dividing the word of truth" (II Tim 2:15).

Notes

Notes

Notes

Speaker: _____ Date: _____

Subject: _____ Place:_____

Main Scripture Texts: _____ _____

Old Testament References

Gen _____	2 Chr_____	Dan _____
Ex _____	Ezra _____	Hos _____
Lev _____	Neh _____	Joel _____
Num _____	Est _____	Amos_____
Dt _____	Job _____	Obad _____
Josh _____	Ps _____	Jon _____
Jud _____	Prov _____	Mic _____
Ruth _____	Eccl _____	Nah _____
1 Sam_____	Song _____	Hab _____
2 Sam_____	Isa _____	Zeph _____
1 Ki _____	Jer _____	Hag _____
2 Ki _____	Lam _____	Zech _____
1 Chr _____	Ezek _____	Mal _____

New Testament References

Mt _____	Eph _____	Heb _____
Mk _____	Phil _____	Jas _____
Lk _____	Col _____	1 Pet _____
Jn _____	1 Th _____	2 Pet _____
Acts _____	2 Th _____	1 Jn _____
Rom _____	1 Tim_____	2 Jn _____
1 Cor_____	2 Tim_____	3 Jn _____
2 Cor_____	Ti _____	Jude _____
Gal _____	Phile _____	Rev _____

"Study to shew thyself approved unto God, a workman that needeth not be ashamed, rightly dividing the word of truth" (II Tim 2:15).

Notes

Notes

Notes

Speaker: _____ Date: _____

Subject: _____ Place: _____

Main Scripture Texts: _____ _____

Old Testament References

Gen	_____	2 Chr	_____	Dan	_____
Ex	_____	Ezra	_____	Hos	_____
Lev	_____	Neh	_____	Joel	_____
Num	_____	Est	_____	Amos	_____
Dt	_____	Job	_____	Obad	_____
Josh	_____	Ps	_____	Jon	_____
Jud	_____	Prov	_____	Mic	_____
Ruth	_____	Eccl	_____	Nah	_____
1 Sam	_____	Song	_____	Hab	_____
2 Sam	_____	Isa	_____	Zeph	_____
1 Ki	_____	Jer	_____	Hag	_____
2 Ki	_____	Lam	_____	Zech	_____
1 Chr	_____	Ezek	_____	Mal	_____

New Testament References

Mt	_____	Eph	_____	Heb	_____
Mk	_____	Phil	_____	Jas	_____
Lk	_____	Col	_____	1 Pet	_____
Jn	_____	1 Th	_____	2 Pet	_____
Acts	_____	2 Th	_____	1 Jn	_____
Rom	_____	1 Tim	_____	2 Jn	_____
1 Cor	_____	2 Tim	_____	3 Jn	_____
2 Cor	_____	Ti	_____	Jude	_____
Gal	_____	Phile	_____	Rev	_____

"Study to shew thyself approved unto God, a workman that needeth not be ashamed, rightly dividing the word of truth" (II Tim 2:15).

Notes

Notes

Notes

Speaker: _____ Date: _____

Subject: _____ Place: _____

Main Scripture Texts: _____ _____

Old Testament References

Gen _____	2 Chr _____	Dan _____
Ex _____	Ezra _____	Hos _____
Lev _____	Neh _____	Joel _____
Num _____	Est _____	Amos _____
Dt _____	Job _____	Obad _____
Josh _____	Ps _____	Jon _____
Jud _____	Prov _____	Mic _____
Ruth _____	Eccl _____	Nah _____
1 Sam _____	Song _____	Hab _____
2 Sam _____	Isa _____	Zeph _____
1 Ki _____	Jer _____	Hag _____
2 Ki _____	Lam _____	Zech _____
1 Chr _____	Ezek _____	Mal _____

New Testament References

Mt _____	Eph _____	Heb _____
Mk _____	Phil _____	Jas _____
Lk _____	Col _____	1 Pet _____
Jn _____	1 Th _____	2 Pet _____
Acts _____	2 Th _____	1 Jn _____
Rom _____	1 Tim _____	2 Jn _____
1 Cor _____	2 Tim _____	3 Jn _____
2 Cor _____	Ti _____	Jude _____
Gal _____	Phile _____	Rev _____

"Study to shew thyself approved unto God, a workman that needeth not be ashamed, rightly dividing the word of truth" (II Tim 2:15).

Notes

Notes

Notes

Speaker: _____ Date: _____

Subject: _____ Place: _____

Main Scripture Texts: _____ _____

Old Testament References

Gen _____	2 Chr_____	Dan _____
Ex _____	Ezra _____	Hos _____
Lev _____	Neh _____	Joel _____
Num _____	Est _____	Amos_____
Dt _____	Job _____	Obad _____
Josh _____	Ps _____	Jon _____
Jud _____	Prov _____	Mic _____
Ruth _____	Eccl _____	Nah _____
1 Sam_____	Song _____	Hab _____
2 Sam_____	Isa _____	Zeph _____
1 Ki _____	Jer _____	Hag _____
2 Ki _____	Lam _____	Zech _____
1 Chr _____	Ezek _____	Mal _____

New Testament References

Mt _____	Eph _____	Heb _____
Mk _____	Phil _____	Jas _____
Lk _____	Col _____	1 Pet _____
Jn _____	1 Th _____	2 Pet _____
Acts _____	2 Th _____	1 Jn _____
Rom _____	1 Tim_____	2 Jn _____
1 Cor_____	2 Tim_____	3 Jn _____
2 Cor_____	Ti _____	Jude _____
Gal _____	Phile _____	Rev _____

"Study to shew thyself approved unto God, a workman that needeth not be ashamed, rightly dividing the word of truth" (II Tim 2:15).

Notes

Notes

Notes

Speaker: _____ Date: _____

Subject: _____ Place: _____

Main Scripture Texts: _____ _____

Old Testament References

Gen _____	2 Chr _____	Dan _____
Ex _____	Ezra _____	Hos _____
Lev _____	Neh _____	Joel _____
Num _____	Est _____	Amos _____
Dt _____	Job _____	Obad _____
Josh _____	Ps _____	Jon _____
Jud _____	Prov _____	Mic _____
Ruth _____	Eccl _____	Nah _____
1 Sam _____	Song _____	Hab _____
2 Sam _____	Isa _____	Zeph _____
1 Ki _____	Jer _____	Hag _____
2 Ki _____	Lam _____	Zech _____
1 Chr _____	Ezek _____	Mal _____

New Testament References

Mt _____	Eph _____	Heb _____
Mk _____	Phil _____	Jas _____
Lk _____	Col _____	1 Pet _____
Jn _____	1 Th _____	2 Pet _____
Acts _____	2 Th _____	1 Jn _____
Rom _____	1 Tim _____	2 Jn _____
1 Cor _____	2 Tim _____	3 Jn _____
2 Cor _____	Ti _____	Jude _____
Gal _____	Phile _____	Rev _____

"Study to shew thyself approved unto God, a workman that needeth not be ashamed, rightly dividing the word of truth" (II Tim 2:15).

Notes

Notes

Notes

Speaker: _____ Date: _____

Subject: _____ Place: _____

Main Scripture Texts: _____ _____

Old Testament References

Gen _____	2 Chr _____	Dan _____
Ex _____	Ezra _____	Hos _____
Lev _____	Neh _____	Joel _____
Num _____	Est _____	Amos _____
Dt _____	Job _____	Obad _____
Josh _____	Ps _____	Jon _____
Jud _____	Prov _____	Mic _____
Ruth _____	Eccl _____	Nah _____
1 Sam _____	Song _____	Hab _____
2 Sam _____	Isa _____	Zeph _____
1 Ki _____	Jer _____	Hag _____
2 Ki _____	Lam _____	Zech _____
1 Chr _____	Ezek _____	Mal _____

New Testament References

Mt _____	Eph _____	Heb _____
Mk _____	Phil _____	Jas _____
Lk _____	Col _____	1 Pet _____
Jn _____	1 Th _____	2 Pet _____
Acts _____	2 Th _____	1 Jn _____
Rom _____	1 Tim _____	2 Jn _____
1 Cor _____	2 Tim _____	3 Jn _____
2 Cor _____	Ti _____	Jude _____
Gal _____	Phile _____	Rev _____

"Study to shew thyself approved unto God, a workman that needeth not be ashamed, rightly dividing the word of truth" (II Tim 2:15).

Notes

Notes

Notes

Speaker: _____ Date: _____

Subject: _____ Place:_____

Main Scripture Texts: _____ _____

Old Testament References

Gen _____	2 Chr_____	Dan _____
Ex _____	Ezra _____	Hos _____
Lev _____	Neh _____	Joel _____
Num _____	Est _____	Amos_____
Dt _____	Job _____	Obad_____
Josh _____	Ps _____	Jon _____
Jud _____	Prov _____	Mic _____
Ruth _____	Eccl _____	Nah _____
1 Sam_____	Song _____	Hab _____
2 Sam_____	Isa _____	Zeph _____
1 Ki _____	Jer _____	Hag _____
2 Ki _____	Lam _____	Zech _____
1 Chr _____	Ezek _____	Mal _____

New Testament References

Mt _____	Eph _____	Heb _____
Mk _____	Phil _____	Jas _____
Lk _____	Col _____	1 Pet _____
Jn _____	1 Th _____	2 Pet _____
Acts _____	2 Th _____	1 Jn _____
Rom _____	1 Tim_____	2 Jn _____
1 Cor_____	2 Tim_____	3 Jn _____
2 Cor_____	Ti _____	Jude _____
Gal _____	Phile _____	Rev _____

"Study to shew thyself approved unto God, a workman that needeth not be ashamed, rightly dividing the word of truth" (II Tim 2:15).

Notes

Notes

<u>Notes</u>

Speaker: _____ Date: _____

Subject: _____ Place:_____

Main Scripture Texts: _____ _____

Old Testament References

Gen _____	2 Chr_____	Dan _____
Ex _____	Ezra _____	Hos _____
Lev _____	Neh _____	Joel _____
Num _____	Est _____	Amos_____
Dt _____	Job _____	Obad _____
Josh _____	Ps _____	Jon _____
Jud _____	Prov _____	Mic _____
Ruth _____	Eccl _____	Nah _____
1 Sam_____	Song _____	Hab _____
2 Sam_____	Isa _____	Zeph _____
1 Ki _____	Jer _____	Hag _____
2 Ki _____	Lam _____	Zech _____
1 Chr _____	Ezek _____	Mal _____

New Testament References

Mt _____	Eph _____	Heb _____
Mk _____	Phil _____	Jas _____
Lk _____	Col _____	1 Pet _____
Jn _____	1 Th _____	2 Pet _____
Acts _____	2 Th _____	1 Jn _____
Rom _____	1 Tim_____	2 Jn _____
1 Cor_____	2 Tim_____	3 Jn _____
2 Cor_____	Ti _____	Jude _____
Gal _____	Phile _____	Rev _____

"Study to shew thyself approved unto God, a workman that needeth not be ashamed, rightly dividing the word of truth" (II Tim 2:15).

Notes

Notes

Notes

Speaker: _____ Date: _____

Subject: _____ Place:_____

Main Scripture Texts: _____ _____

Old Testament References

Gen	_____	2 Chr	_____	Dan	_____
Ex	_____	Ezra	_____	Hos	_____
Lev	_____	Neh	_____	Joel	_____
Num	_____	Est	_____	Amos	_____
Dt	_____	Job	_____	Obad	_____
Josh	_____	Ps	_____	Jon	_____
Jud	_____	Prov	_____	Mic	_____
Ruth	_____	Eccl	_____	Nah	_____
1 Sam	_____	Song	_____	Hab	_____
2 Sam	_____	Isa	_____	Zeph	_____
1 Ki	_____	Jer	_____	Hag	_____
2 Ki	_____	Lam	_____	Zech	_____
1 Chr	_____	Ezek	_____	Mal	_____

New Testament References

Mt	_____	Eph	_____	Heb	_____
Mk	_____	Phil	_____	Jas	_____
Lk	_____	Col	_____	1 Pet	_____
Jn	_____	1 Th	_____	2 Pet	_____
Acts	_____	2 Th	_____	1 Jn	_____
Rom	_____	1 Tim	_____	2 Jn	_____
1 Cor	_____	2 Tim	_____	3 Jn	_____
2 Cor	_____	Ti	_____	Jude	_____
Gal	_____	Phile	_____	Rev	_____

"Study to shew thyself approved unto God, a workman that needeth not be ashamed, rightly dividing the word of truth" (II Tim 2:15).

Notes

Notes

Notes

Speaker: _____ Date: _____

Subject: _____ Place:_____

Main Scripture Texts: _____ _____

Old Testament References

Gen _____	2 Chr_____	Dan _____
Ex _____	Ezra _____	Hos _____
Lev _____	Neh _____	Joel _____
Num _____	Est _____	Amos_____
Dt _____	Job _____	Obad _____
Josh _____	Ps _____	Jon _____
Jud _____	Prov _____	Mic _____
Ruth _____	Eccl _____	Nah _____
1 Sam_____	Song _____	Hab _____
2 Sam_____	Isa _____	Zeph _____
1 Ki _____	Jer _____	Hag _____
2 Ki _____	Lam _____	Zech _____
1 Chr _____	Ezek _____	Mal _____

New Testament References

Mt _____	Eph _____	Heb _____
Mk _____	Phil _____	Jas _____
Lk _____	Col _____	1 Pet _____
Jn _____	1 Th _____	2 Pet _____
Acts _____	2 Th _____	1 Jn _____
Rom _____	1 Tim_____	2 Jn _____
1 Cor_____	2 Tim_____	3 Jn _____
2 Cor_____	Ti _____	Jude _____
Gal _____	Phile _____	Rev _____

"Study to shew thyself approved unto God, a workman that needeth not be ashamed, rightly dividing the word of truth" (II Tim 2:15).

Notes

Notes

Notes

Speaker: _____ Date: _____

Subject: _____ Place:_____

Main Scripture Texts: _____ _____

Old Testament References

Gen _____	2 Chr_____	Dan _____
Ex _____	Ezra _____	Hos _____
Lev _____	Neh _____	Joel _____
Num _____	Est _____	Amos_____
Dt _____	Job _____	Obad _____
Josh _____	Ps _____	Jon _____
Jud _____	Prov _____	Mic _____
Ruth _____	Eccl _____	Nah _____
1 Sam_____	Song _____	Hab _____
2 Sam_____	Isa _____	Zeph _____
1 Ki _____	Jer _____	Hag _____
2 Ki _____	Lam _____	Zech _____
1 Chr _____	Ezek _____	Mal _____

New Testament References

Mt _____	Eph _____	Heb _____
Mk _____	Phil _____	Jas _____
Lk _____	Col _____	1 Pet _____
Jn _____	1 Th _____	2 Pet _____
Acts _____	2 Th _____	1 Jn _____
Rom _____	1 Tim_____	2 Jn _____
1 Cor_____	2 Tim_____	3 Jn _____
2 Cor_____	Ti _____	Jude _____
Gal _____	Phile _____	Rev _____

"Study to shew thyself approved unto God, a workman that needeth not be ashamed, rightly dividing the word of truth" (II Tim 2:15).

Notes

Notes

Notes

Speaker: _____ Date: _____

Subject: _____ Place: _____

Main Scripture Texts: _____ _____

Old Testament References

Gen	_____	2 Chr	_____	Dan	_____
Ex	_____	Ezra	_____	Hos	_____
Lev	_____	Neh	_____	Joel	_____
Num	_____	Est	_____	Amos	_____
Dt	_____	Job	_____	Obad	_____
Josh	_____	Ps	_____	Jon	_____
Jud	_____	Prov	_____	Mic	_____
Ruth	_____	Eccl	_____	Nah	_____
1 Sam	_____	Song	_____	Hab	_____
2 Sam	_____	Isa	_____	Zeph	_____
1 Ki	_____	Jer	_____	Hag	_____
2 Ki	_____	Lam	_____	Zech	_____
1 Chr	_____	Ezek	_____	Mal	_____

New Testament References

Mt	_____	Eph	_____	Heb	_____
Mk	_____	Phil	_____	Jas	_____
Lk	_____	Col	_____	1 Pet	_____
Jn	_____	1 Th	_____	2 Pet	_____
Acts	_____	2 Th	_____	1 Jn	_____
Rom	_____	1 Tim	_____	2 Jn	_____
1 Cor	_____	2 Tim	_____	3 Jn	_____
2 Cor	_____	Ti	_____	Jude	_____
Gal	_____	Phile	_____	Rev	_____

"Study to shew thyself approved unto God, a workman that needeth not be ashamed, rightly dividing the word of truth" (II Tim 2:15).

Notes

Notes

Notes

Speaker: _____   Date: _____

Subject: _____   Place: _____

Main Scripture Texts: _____   _____

Old Testament References

Gen	_____	2 Chr	_____	Dan	_____
Ex	_____	Ezra	_____	Hos	_____
Lev	_____	Neh	_____	Joel	_____
Num	_____	Est	_____	Amos	_____
Dt	_____	Job	_____	Obad	_____
Josh	_____	Ps	_____	Jon	_____
Jud	_____	Prov	_____	Mic	_____
Ruth	_____	Eccl	_____	Nah	_____
1 Sam	_____	Song	_____	Hab	_____
2 Sam	_____	Isa	_____	Zeph	_____
1 Ki	_____	Jer	_____	Hag	_____
2 Ki	_____	Lam	_____	Zech	_____
1 Chr	_____	Ezek	_____	Mal	_____

New Testament References

Mt	_____	Eph	_____	Heb	_____
Mk	_____	Phil	_____	Jas	_____
Lk	_____	Col	_____	1 Pet	_____
Jn	_____	1 Th	_____	2 Pet	_____
Acts	_____	2 Th	_____	1 Jn	_____
Rom	_____	1 Tim	_____	2 Jn	_____
1 Cor	_____	2 Tim	_____	3 Jn	_____
2 Cor	_____	Ti	_____	Jude	_____
Gal	_____	Phile	_____	Rev	_____

"Study to shew thyself approved unto God, a workman that needeth not be ashamed, rightly dividing the word of truth" (II Tim 2:15).

Notes

Notes

Notes

Speaker: _____ Date: _____

Subject: _____ Place:_____

Main Scripture Texts: _____ _____

Old Testament References

Gen _____	2 Chr _____	Dan _____
Ex _____	Ezra _____	Hos _____
Lev _____	Neh _____	Joel _____
Num _____	Est _____	Amos_____
Dt _____	Job _____	Obad _____
Josh _____	Ps _____	Jon _____
Jud _____	Prov _____	Mic _____
Ruth _____	Eccl _____	Nah _____
1 Sam_____	Song _____	Hab _____
2 Sam_____	Isa _____	Zeph _____
1 Ki _____	Jer _____	Hag _____
2 Ki _____	Lam _____	Zech _____
1 Chr _____	Ezek _____	Mal _____

New Testament References

Mt _____	Eph _____	Heb _____
Mk _____	Phil _____	Jas _____
Lk _____	Col _____	1 Pet _____
Jn _____	1 Th _____	2 Pet _____
Acts _____	2 Th _____	1 Jn _____
Rom _____	1 Tim_____	2 Jn _____
1 Cor_____	2 Tim_____	3 Jn _____
2 Cor_____	Ti _____	Jude _____
Gal _____	Phile _____	Rev _____

"Study to shew thyself approved unto God, a workman that needeth not be ashamed, rightly dividing the word of truth" (II Tim 2:15).

Notes

<u>Notes</u>

Notes

Speaker: _____ Date: _____

Subject: _____ Place:_____

Main Scripture Texts: _____ _____

Old Testament References

Gen _____	2 Chr _____	Dan _____
Ex _____	Ezra _____	Hos _____
Lev _____	Neh _____	Joel _____
Num _____	Est _____	Amos_____
Dt _____	Job _____	Obad _____
Josh _____	Ps _____	Jon _____
Jud _____	Prov _____	Mic _____
Ruth _____	Eccl _____	Nah _____
1 Sam_____	Song _____	Hab _____
2 Sam_____	Isa _____	Zeph _____
1 Ki _____	Jer _____	Hag _____
2 Ki _____	Lam _____	Zech _____
1 Chr _____	Ezek _____	Mal _____

New Testament References

Mt _____	Eph _____	Heb _____
Mk _____	Phil _____	Jas _____
Lk _____	Col _____	1 Pet _____
Jn _____	1 Th _____	2 Pet _____
Acts _____	2 Th _____	1 Jn _____
Rom _____	1 Tim_____	2 Jn _____
1 Cor _____	2 Tim_____	3 Jn _____
2 Cor _____	Ti _____	Jude _____
Gal _____	Phile _____	Rev _____

"Study to shew thyself approved unto God, a workman that needeth not be ashamed, rightly dividing the word of truth" (II Tim 2:15).

Notes

Notes

Notes

Speaker: _____ Date: _____

Subject: _____ Place: _____

Main Scripture Texts: _____ _____

Old Testament References

Gen _____	2 Chr_____	Dan _____
Ex _____	Ezra _____	Hos _____
Lev _____	Neh _____	Joel _____
Num _____	Est _____	Amos_____
Dt _____	Job _____	Obad _____
Josh _____	Ps _____	Jon _____
Jud _____	Prov _____	Mic _____
Ruth _____	Eccl _____	Nah _____
1 Sam_____	Song _____	Hab _____
2 Sam_____	Isa _____	Zeph _____
1 Ki _____	Jer _____	Hag _____
2 Ki _____	Lam _____	Zech _____
1 Chr_____	Ezek _____	Mal _____

New Testament References

Mt _____	Eph _____	Heb _____
Mk _____	Phil _____	Jas _____
Lk _____	Col _____	1 Pet _____
Jn _____	1 Th _____	2 Pet _____
Acts _____	2 Th _____	1 Jn _____
Rom _____	1 Tim_____	2 Jn _____
1 Cor_____	2 Tim_____	3 Jn _____
2 Cor_____	Ti _____	Jude _____
Gal _____	Phile _____	Rev _____

"Study to shew thyself approved unto God, a workman that needeth not be ashamed, rightly dividing the word of truth" (II Tim 2:15).

Notes

Notes

Notes

Speaker: _____ Date: _____

Subject: _____ Place:_____

Main Scripture Texts: _____ _____

Old Testament References

Gen	_____	2 Chr	_____	Dan	_____
Ex	_____	Ezra	_____	Hos	_____
Lev	_____	Neh	_____	Joel	_____
Num	_____	Est	_____	Amos	_____
Dt	_____	Job	_____	Obad	_____
Josh	_____	Ps	_____	Jon	_____
Jud	_____	Prov	_____	Mic	_____
Ruth	_____	Eccl	_____	Nah	_____
1 Sam	_____	Song	_____	Hab	_____
2 Sam	_____	Isa	_____	Zeph	_____
1 Ki	_____	Jer	_____	Hag	_____
2 Ki	_____	Lam	_____	Zech	_____
1 Chr	_____	Ezek	_____	Mal	_____

New Testament References

Mt	_____	Eph	_____	Heb	_____
Mk	_____	Phil	_____	Jas	_____
Lk	_____	Col	_____	1 Pet	_____
Jn	_____	1 Th	_____	2 Pet	_____
Acts	_____	2 Th	_____	1 Jn	_____
Rom	_____	1 Tim	_____	2 Jn	_____
1 Cor	_____	2 Tim	_____	3 Jn	_____
2 Cor	_____	Ti	_____	Jude	_____
Gal	_____	Phile	_____	Rev	_____

"Study to shew thyself approved unto God, a workman that needeth not be ashamed, rightly dividing the word of truth" (II Tim 2:15).

Notes

Notes

Notes

Speaker: _____ Date: _____

Subject: _____ Place: _____

Main Scripture Texts: _____ _____

Old Testament References

Gen _____	2 Chr _____	Dan _____
Ex _____	Ezra _____	Hos _____
Lev _____	Neh _____	Joel _____
Num _____	Est _____	Amos _____
Dt _____	Job _____	Obad _____
Josh _____	Ps _____	Jon _____
Jud _____	Prov _____	Mic _____
Ruth _____	Eccl _____	Nah _____
1 Sam _____	Song _____	Hab _____
2 Sam _____	Isa _____	Zeph _____
1 Ki _____	Jer _____	Hag _____
2 Ki _____	Lam _____	Zech _____
1 Chr _____	Ezek _____	Mal _____

New Testament References

Mt _____	Eph _____	Heb _____
Mk _____	Phil _____	Jas _____
Lk _____	Col _____	1 Pet _____
Jn _____	1 Th _____	2 Pet _____
Acts _____	2 Th _____	1 Jn _____
Rom _____	1 Tim _____	2 Jn _____
1 Cor _____	2 Tim _____	3 Jn _____
2 Cor _____	Ti _____	Jude _____
Gal _____	Phile _____	Rev _____

"Study to shew thyself approved unto God, a workman that needeth not be ashamed, rightly dividing the word of truth" (II Tim 2:15).

Notes

Notes

Notes

Speaker: _____ Date: _____

Subject: _____ Place: _____

Main Scripture Texts: _____ _____

Old Testament References

Gen _____	2 Chr _____	Dan _____
Ex _____	Ezra _____	Hos _____
Lev _____	Neh _____	Joel _____
Num _____	Est _____	Amos _____
Dt _____	Job _____	Obad _____
Josh _____	Ps _____	Jon _____
Jud _____	Prov _____	Mic _____
Ruth _____	Eccl _____	Nah _____
1 Sam _____	Song _____	Hab _____
2 Sam _____	Isa _____	Zeph _____
1 Ki _____	Jer _____	Hag _____
2 Ki _____	Lam _____	Zech _____
1 Chr _____	Ezek _____	Mal _____

New Testament References

Mt _____	Eph _____	Heb _____
Mk _____	Phil _____	Jas _____
Lk _____	Col _____	1 Pet _____
Jn _____	1 Th _____	2 Pet _____
Acts _____	2 Th _____	1 Jn _____
Rom _____	1 Tim _____	2 Jn _____
1 Cor _____	2 Tim _____	3 Jn _____
2 Cor _____	Ti _____	Jude _____
Gal _____	Phile _____	Rev _____

"Study to shew thyself approved unto God, a workman that needeth not be ashamed, rightly dividing the word of truth" (II Tim 2:15).

Notes

Notes

Notes

❧ _People to Remember_ ☙

Name	Phone

ઉ _People to Remember_ ભ

Name	Phone

Scriptures to Remember

Anger	Mt 5:22, 1 Pet 2:23, Eph 4:26, ITh 5:9
Anxiety	Phil 4:7, Isa 32:17, Jn 14:27, Job 11:18-19
Backsliding	Prov 28:13, Ps 51:10-12, Jn 6:37
Bereavement/Grief	Mt 5:22, Isa 51:12, Prov 10:22, Ps 119:50
Bitterness	Eph 4:31, Heb 12:15, James 3:14-15
Carnality	Rom 6:6-9, Eph 4:22-24, 2 Cor 4:16
Condemnation	Rom 8:1, Rom 3:24, Rom 8:30, Acts 13:39
Confusion	Isa 30:21, Psa 25:9, Psa 48:14, Psa 37:5,23
Death	Rom 14:7-8, Job 19:25-27, Isa 55:8-9
Depression	Neh 8:10, Phil 4:8, Rom 8:28
Direction	Prov 3:6, Psa 37:23, Isa 30:21, Psa 37:5, Psa 73:24
Dissatisfaction	Prov 27:20, Heb 13:5-6, 1Tim 6:6-8
Doubt	Phil 4:13, 2 Cor 3:5, Rom 4:21, Heb 10:23, Psa 89:34
Fear	Psa 112:7, 2 Pet 3:9, 2 Cor 1:20, Job 22:27 Psa 34 :17
Finances	Phil 4:19, Lk 11:9, Lk 12:24, Mt 6:32, Psa 84:11
God's Love	Jn 3:16, Rom 5:8
Holiness	1Tim 4:8, Rom 12:2, Phil 4:7, Jas 4:8, Jer 6:16
Insecurity	Dt 33:27, Psa 46:1, Prov 14:26, Psa 28:8, Phil 4:13,
Judging	1Cor 4:5, Mt 7:3-5, Jn 5:22
Loneliness	Heb 13:5, Isa 54:10, 1 Jn 1:3, Prov 18:24, Rev 3:20
Lust	2 Pet 2:9, Mt 18:8-9, Prov 6: 25-26
Marriage	2 Cor 6:14-17, 1Cor 7:10-17, Heb 13:4
Pride	Mt 18:2-4, Pro 27:1-2, Lk 18:11-14
Salvation	Rev 3:20, Rom 10:13
Satan	Eph 6:10-17, 1Jn 4:1-3, Lk 10:18-19
Sickness:	Jas 5:14-16, Mk 16:17-18, Jer 30:17, Psa 41:3, 2Cor 4:17
Sin	Rom 3:23, Rom 3:10, Rom 6:23, 1Cor 15:3-4
Suffering	Heb 5:8-9, 2 Cor 4:8-10, 1 Pet 4:19
Temptation	Rom 8:37, 1 Cor 10:13, 2 Pet 2:9, Heb 2:18, 2 Cor 12:9
Trials	2 Tim 2:3, 1 Pet 4:12-13, Psa 34:17, Rev 2:10
Weakness	2 Cor 12:9, Mt 11:28-30, Psa 121:2-3
Wisdom	Jas 1:5, Eccl 2:26, 1 Cor 2:14-15, Psa 16:7, Prov 2: 6-7
Worldliness	Mk 4: 18-20, 1 Jn 5:5, 1 John 2:15-17